Poetry and Reflection

By Roger Neumaier

Table of Contents:

A Note about *Poetry and Reflection*

I retired in January of 2014, ready to focus upon my lifelong ambition of writing. In addition to literary fiction, I decided to write at least one poem a month that reflected my life and the world around me.

The intervening years have been meaningful, but also full of pain. Between February of 2015 and March of 2017, my life was changed by the deaths of my father, my mother, my step-mother and my wife.

I did not review these poems until 2022. At that time, I saw how my attitudes had changed and grown during the years reflected in this volume.

I hope you will find this poetry collection to be meaningful.

Roger Neumaier

I am Retired

February 17, 2014

The beginning of new things,
The end of a certain slavery.
My tank was empty and
I will no longer ignore that
To press forward.

In its place,
I have the opportunity for emptiness
(And whatever springs from that).
I now have time
For quiet
And the percolation of new perspectives.

This celebration of peace
Is not what I targeted
In the nineteen-sixties
As I ventured into adulthood
Sporting long hair and worn blue jeans.

But I am ready
And oh, so thankful for my health.

My Grandparents

February 19, 2014

I remember my grandparents
Throughout the years—
Always loving, generous and giving.

I remember the smells
Of my grandpa's cigars,
And my grandmother's pies;
The chaos in their home
When family visited;
And the peace when it was just the three of us.

I remember sitting on the couch,
My grandma on my left, my grandpa on my right,
And me—holding that photo album—in between.
That album captured special moments,
Snapshots that preceded my birth
By decades.

My grandparents gave me so much love!
I will never forget them
Nor those special moments.

Quiet

February 20, 2014

I enjoy the quiet
Following all those years
Of too much noise.

Doing nothing does raise my guilt.
But I did too much
For too long,
(Always efficiently).
This nothingness feels good—
Like a hot bath.

A hot bath is safe and secure nothingness.
After washing and scrubbing,
Doing nothing
In the comfort of hot water
Is mesmerizing.

The fear,
Of course,
Is that I will never again do anything of consequence.

But that is the risk I take.

Primitive 2014

February 20, 2014

Primitive man captured fire,
Found shelter (or made it),
Hunted for food,
Scavenged for clothing,
But was often cold, hungry and afraid.

Today, we buy all of our things.
Our fear has become loss of buying power.
Our hunt occurs at a mall.

Are we better off
Or have we just become insulated from the truth?

Updating Saturday Mornings

February 22, 2014

When I was a child,
Saturday morning
Was a time for TV westerns
And an assortment of cartoons.

As I grew older,
Saturday morning became my time for relaxing,
I'd read the paper, drink coffee
And complete projects around the house.

As I aged, my parents did as well.
After I'd read the newspaper and drunk my coffee,
I'd speak with my father on the phone,
Then drive over to take care of my mother.
Those tasks complete, I tried to rest,
Exhausted from a workweek of chaos
And preparing for the next one.

Now that I am retired.
Life is easier.
I am not as tired.
I drink my coffee, read my paper,
And ask myself
How shall I spend the day?

Saturday mornings are still special.

Putting my Workshop in Order
February 27, 2014

My workshop was a mess.
(It reflected the chaos of my soul).
But I wanted to start a project.
I stood in front of the workbench.
But instead of putting each tool where it belonged,
I imagined changing the workshop,
Taking out that counter and
Moving things that never belonged in my workshop
Into other rooms.

One item at a time,
I am reshaping that room,
Moving tools around,
Putting the workshop
And my life
Into order—
Creating a much-needed serenity.

I have only started
This tool room restructure.
But my spirit soars
As I anticipate
Going down to the workshop
For my next project.

Settling In

March 20, 2014

It has been almost seven weeks
Since I retired.
There are no regrets.
Life is slower
And better.

I embraced
Winter passed into spring.
I had a fresh new criterion for life.
The goals, objectives and strategies,
Which had seemed so important for forty years,
Are no longer necessary.
Individual moments must be my focus.

Life has given me something new.
I am savoring it
As if it were a crystal goblet of Chateau Neuf du Pape.

Changing Gears

March 30, 2014

How to operate a vehicle with a manual transmission:

Maintain pressure on the gas
While pushing in the clutch.
Quickly reduce that pressure and
Move the stick shift to the next gear.
Then, slowly press in the gas pedal,
While letting out the clutch.
Once securely in the next gear,
Accelerate.

Where am I in this process
As I change the gears of my life?

The stick shift is in place
And I am slowly letting out the clutch.

So far,
No gears are grinding.

France
April 26, 2014

A trip to France:
Two weeks enjoying Dordogne, Normandy and Paris;
The caves, castles, battlefields and beauty;
The wine, truffles, foie gras and pastry.
Pushing ourselves, we enjoyed it all.

As I walked the streets of Paris,
I reminisced about my grand youthful adventure.
I realized
I am no longer that young man
Who ventured off to France
Forty years ago
With $500 in his pocket,
Without a job.
But I found work in the City of Light
And loved
Mes six mois a' Paris.

Oh yes.
Life is a continuously changing
Set of circumstances.

Musings on Prehistory

June 3, 2014

A whimsical dream
Of not having to go to work
Has become my reality.

Summer vacation always?
Perhaps.

However,
The guilt of having such a sweet life
Is paired with the responsibility
Of spending it wisely.

What does that mean?

Seventeen-thousand years ago,
It meant climbing into a cave
To draw pictures of deer and buffalo.

Where is my cave?

A Big Need for Reformation
June 6, 2014

My dad gave me a subscription to *The Nation*,
A radical periodical that employs large words
To describe an ideal world.

Could its authors
Use simpler sentences
To communicate their ideas?

No.
Of course not!

Their intellects manage concepts
That are just too multifaceted
For less sophisticated minds.

Perhaps,
After the revolution,
The radial intellects of the world
Will find a way to connect
With the workers of the world.

D-Day Remembered

June 6, 2014

Now,
Seventy years later,
We remember the sheer magnitude
Of the challenge
Those young men faced
As they threw their bodies
Against the armaments of the Fuhrer.

What if D-Day hadn't happened?
What if those young farmers, mechanics,
Teachers and students
Had not been called to a higher challenge—
Or had not responded?
What then?

Fortunately,
That question is theoretical.

Today, as mankind lumbers forward.
We wait breathlessly
For a new Eisenhower
On a new D-Day
To marshal our forces.
On that day,
We will not be rescuing democracy.
We will be trying to save our planet.

Life as a Chess Game

June 15, 2014

Chess is a simple game
Played on a simple board—
Black and white pieces
In a black and white world.

I patiently examine the board,
Taking my time
Before making my move.
Alternative opportunities have been visualized,
Diverse outcomes imagined,
Moves that got me to this point considered,
As were the objectives they embraced.

In real life,
However,
Your life can go to hell
After a single move.

But in chess,
There is no risk.
It is all about
Learning to think cleanly
And clearly
While discovering peace
In the midst of a game of war.

My Dream

June 27, 2014

My dream has always been to write.

In my professional life,
I wrote many complex analyses—
They were clear,
Well-reasoned,
And reached strong conclusions.

While I was under no illusion
That I had fulfilled my dream,
I earned a living.

Now
I have the time
To write
Each day.

My criteria for success
Have changed.
They are now found in my heart.

Perspectives

July 9, 2014

Postulate:
What we see is a result of how we view a subject.

Does the difference between
Funny and sad;
Interesting and boring;
Pain and pleasure;
Beauty and ugliness; or
Love and hate
Really come down
To the lens
Through which we gaze?

If that is the case,
Then we not only select our subject,
But we imbue it
With the qualities
Upon which it will be judged.

Dementia

July 30, 2014

My mother's mind
Slowly
Began to lose the ability
To process her world.

Points A, B and C
Were not connected.
They no longer formed a line.
Instead, they became disparate events.

But when point A disappeared,
my mother felt betrayed
By God, by nature
And by the people she loved.

This is a world in which there are no soft landings.
We all eventually die.
There are many paths to that death.

Dementia is one powerful poison.
However, once this poison has taken hold,
The sharp edges of reality and
The understanding of what is being lost,
Disappear.

The Dream Team

August 6, 2014

God pulled the team together.
"Your assignment" God said, "is clear.
When humans sleep,
Let their minds frolic.
Embroider imageries of their experience
Into their silent slumber
By threading the needle of their intellect
With the soft thread of their imagination.
Let's call these creations *Dreams*."

Members of the committee
Listened intently.
One committee member said,
"Let's make dreams seem like shadows,
Shadows that are impressionistic images of reality."

Another member added,
"And make the dreams seem utterly fantastic—
Yet real."

The committee members became animated.
Dreams would be metaphors!
Woven into the fabric of the dream
Would be joy, sadness, fear, anger and anticipation.

(continued on next page)

(Dream Team continued)

The committee's prankster added,
"When a dreamer wakes,
Let's have their dream seem totally memorable.
But slowly fade away,
Like a sunset disappearing into the horizon."

The committee chair banged her gavel and said,
"Let the minutes show
That the committee has adopted this plan
And this committee is now dissolved."

Aches and Pains

September 27, 2014

My shoulder hurts.
My neck hurts.
My right thumb hurts.
And, my left wrist is in pain.

My back is sore across my hips
And every other part of me aches.

So, why am I going out
Into the garden
To move the Japanese Maple?

The Hunt

October 13, 2014

We no longer walk through the forest
With a spear
Ready to kill a deer, shoot a goose,
Or trap some other animal.

We don't rise early in the morning
To catch a largemouth bass
Or walk through the forest
Digging up roots and searching for mushrooms.

No.
Our adventures have changed.
We wake up early the day after Thanksgiving,
To drive to Walmart to purchase a cheap TV.
We study on-line advertisements
Looking for great deals
With free shipping.

And afterwards,
We stuff our faces with large burgers and fries,
Celebrating a successful hunt.
Our instincts haven't gone away.
They just serve us in a new sphere
As the consumers we have become.

(continued on next page)

Poetry and Reflection

(The Hunt continued)

But what will happen next?
When we are no longer hungry,
When our home is crowded with acquisitions,
And we have the newest automobile?
What happens when we don't want more?

Don't worry.
We'll want more.

Time and Space

December 23, 2014

Time Passes.
But how one fills one's time—
Therein lies the art:
Which task one chooses
(Or doesn't choose)
To include
In one's array of efforts;
How thoroughly one decides to attack each task;
What sort of perfection one pursues;
When and why.

These decisions represent the art of life.

Sufficient palettes of paint exist
To thoroughly cover any canvas.
But the Japanese artist has shown us
That a painting
Will be more complete
When it includes
The appropriate amount of space.

Thin as a Rail

January 3, 2015

As a child,
I ate whatever I liked,
Whenever I liked,
And as much as I wanted.

I didn't think about it
When I was
Chasing friends in a field
Or watching television.
It made no difference.
I was thin as a rail.

But as I have aged,
Things have changed.

I've learned to eat fewer snacks,
Better foods
In smaller portions.

Still, the days when I was thin as a rail are gone—
Not to return until I recline
In my own pine box.

The Big Clock

February 18, 2015

Time passes.

The pharaohs tried to assure
A journey to another world.
The Christians try to pretend
That life is an hors d'oeuvre
Prior to a grand feast.

Yet that big clock keeps ticking.

Each of us will one day disappear,
And be forgotten.

For what purpose?

Satisfaction

March 16, 2015

Connecting what you have
To what you want;
Turning potential
Into reality;
Crafting a plan and
Executing it.

Begin with hunger or thirst,
Need or desire,
Hope or anticipation;
Then pursue completion.

Without emptiness,
There can be no fulfillment.
Without desire,
There can be no satisfaction.

Perspectives

May 15, 2015

Each person's view is unique.
There are many different ways
To see what is around us.

And yet,
We are surprised
When others' perception
Is unlike our own.

How can that be?

Wars are fought.
Anger is unleashed.
Disrespect is common
And we regard others as ignorant.

All this because perspectives differ.

How foolish.
How tragic.

Motivation

May 27, 2015

What motivates us
Beyond greed and insecurity?

Is it ego?
Is it a search for validation of self-worth?
Is it the desire to define who we are?
Might it be a search
For confirmation of our existence
Within the continuum of history?

Why do some keep pushing
While others rest?

Why did one man go to the moon,
While another tended his garden,
And a third watched television
As he reclined on his couch?

Solitaire and Life

May 31, 2015

In the game of solitaire,
We can replay the hand we were dealt.
Or we can manipulate the order of the cards
And thus, change the underlying order.
In this way, there are countless ways to win.

But in life,
Facts cannot be changed.
Moves cannot be taken back.
Ominous decisions often must be made
Blindly,
Without understanding
Their consequences.

The End Game

June 1, 2015

So, what is the objective?
What do we live for?
Power, happiness and luxury;
Satisfaction, peace and adventure; or
Safety, security and survival?

Should we pursue
Understanding, knowledge and intellect?
Are we after
Notoriety, wealth and recognition?
Is our objective
Prominence, fame and adoration; or maybe
Creativity, imagination and originality?

What are we pursuing?
Victories, respect and honor;
Cultivation, sophistication and social graces;
Physical health, sensual gratification and sexual
conquest;
Living in the moment, laughter and celebration; or
Piety, wisdom, and salvation?

(continued on next page)

Poetry and Reflection

(The End Game continued)

Each of us must decide
What we are after.
That decision becomes
The declaration of who we are.

Bubbie, Rye Toast, Butter and Jam

June 9, 2015

My breakfast was a piece of rye toast,
Bathed in butter
And smothered with raspberry jam.
Then, I heated up a cup of coffee
To wash down the toast.
As I tasted my breakfast,
I wanted to call my grandmother
And tell her about my rye toast, butter and jam.

She would have understood.
She would have appreciated it.

We called my grandma *Bubbie*.
Bubbie always immersed herself
In the extraordinary richness of life.

I miss Bubbie.
On the day she died twenty-six years ago,
The world became a different place.

Now, I have no one to tell
About the exquisite pleasure
I find in rye toast, butter and raspberry jam.

Decisions

July 9, 2015

When to get up?
What to eat?
What to do?

Throughout the day
I am blessed—
Or plagued—
By the requirement to make decisions.

What to expect?
What to say?
How to react?

So many choices.

Those who are bored,
Those who deny free will and
Those who feel trapped—
They amuse me.

Life is a never-ending maze which
Constantly requiring decisions.

The Zen Garden

July 23, 2015

When I was younger,
I understood the concept
Of gardening
As a Zen exercise.

I understood it
As well as a dictionary
Can define a word.

But really,
How can weeding a garden
Be enlightening?

As I aged,
I have come to understand
That Zen is not a garden.

Zen is the mind
And the way
Of a gardener.

The garden—
It is life.
And oh,
By the way,
There are plenty of weeds.

Focal Point vs. Purpose

July 27, 2015

The focal point is the conclusion
Which you pursue.
It is the destination for your journey,
The outcome you want to achieve.
The focal point is what you envisioned
When you began your effort.

Purpose is the reason
For selecting
A focal point.

Without a focal point,
Or a series of focal points,
You will never achieve
Your purpose.

Without a purpose,
You are a machine
That will eventually burn out.

Modern Times

July 27, 2015

I entertain myself
Pondering modern civilization.

What are we trying to achieve?
Wealth, security, power, conquest,
Cultural richness, salvation or peace?

And for whom?
The wealthy, the powerful, the rich,
The humble, the gentle, the aggressive,
The holy, the confident or the timid?

I haven't answered those questions.
But I have come to understand
Why we select
Arrogant self-centered people as our leaders.

They are never distracted
By those subtleties of life.

Boredom

August 15, 2015

I have always considered boredom
To be a sin
—not a terrible sin
—just a waste-of-part-of-your-life type sin.

So many wonderful paths,
So many opportunities
Are always available.

And yet,
There are those
Who express the belief
That there is nothing to do.

To these people, I say,
Open your eyes!
See the pain in the world.
Recognize how fortunate you are.
Take a step, a taste, a view.
Listen, feel, enjoy and learn.
An extraordinary world is in front of you
Waiting to be discovered.
It can be your personal adventure.

A Dog's Logic

September 22, 2015

I often wonder
About canine logic.
Dogs' enthusiasm
(Or aggression)
Defies understanding.

They anticipate
That they will receive a treat
Every time they enter the house;
That their master or mistress
Will always be there; or
That someday,
The postman will attack.

After their enthusiastic responses,
They lay down,
Resting,
Waiting,
For the next profound awakening of instinct.

I would be much more critical
In my judgement of dogs
If the human race
Weren't so similar.

Life

October 18, 2015

Coming and going;
Acquiring and divesting;
Growing and retracting;
Expressing anger, love and Joy;
Living and dying;
These are all facets of humanity.

We struggle,
Hoping to move forward,
While having little insight
Into where we are going.

Our myths and belief systems
Were constructed in thin air
As a means of insulating us
From the empty feeling
Of recognizing how little we understand.

So,
We spend much of our lives
Focused on *how*.
Because, in truth,
We know nothing about *why*.

Trappings

December 7, 2015

We spend much of our lives—
Much of our energy—
Acquiring trappings.

Do these ornaments
Give us the feeling
Of luxury?
Accomplishment?
Purpose?

I don't know.

But we pursue them
With resolute intensity.

Perhaps we call them trappings
Because our ancestors
Found the same sense of achievement
In their lairs—
Using their captured prey for food and clothing.

Or, on the other hand,
Maybe we are the objects
That have fallen into a trap.

Too Many Things

December 28, 2015

Tools, clothing, furniture and art are fun to purchase.
They make our homes and lives
Comfortable, stylish and complete.

After acquiring them,
Having spent our hard-earned cash
We experience closure—completeness.

But I have always wondered
Why supposedly emotionally healthy people
Continue this pursuit
After filling countless rooms
With innumerable objects.

Why is it still called satisfaction
When should it be labeled meaningless gluttony?

How much happiness
Does a pig experience
Before becoming
Bloated and indolent?

Critical Challenges

December 31, 2015

Life presents us with critical challenges.
From what source?
We don't know.
To what end?
That too is a mystery.

But we do know
We make decisions every day—
Driven by principle, by desire, by ambition
Or by hope.
Some choices lead us to growth,
Others make us smaller.

What is the end game?
How can we evaluate how well we responded?
Who we have become?

Those decisions that occurred
In the face of fear or desire
End up defining us.
How we respond
To those critical challenges
Is our legacy.

Going Slow

January 20, 2016

I was always proud
Of my pace,
Of the speed
With which I could complete a task.

But as I age,
I move more slowly.
I have learned
That thinking something through,
Doing it better,
And enjoying it more
Is worthwhile.

My body cannot move
As lithely as once it could.
But that is not an issue.
I do things once now—
Without jury-rigged corrections
That once were required
To compensate
For my haste.

Quality vs. Quantity

January, 20, 2016

How shall I measure
What I do in my life?

Shall I count the number of accomplishments?
How much I produced,
How great was my accumulation
And how many people were impressed?

Or should I focus
On one act—
One creation—
One detail at a time—
Trying to do that task well?

I guess there is a place
For each approach.

But in the end,
I need to accept
That what is done without quality
Will not last.

Leap Year
February 29, 2016

We mark time
Using arbitrary systems
That integrate (more or less)
With natural cycles.

Sometimes,
We need to adjust our systems—
A quarter of a second here,
A minute there,
A day today—
All to assure
Our somewhat inexact systems
Work.

The only certainty,
However,
Is that the current moment
Will always be the jumping off point
For where we want to go,
Whatever we want to do,
For however long that lasts,
And whatever outcome
Greets us
In the end.

Learning
March 28, 2016

A flower begins with a seed.
It expands
Adding roots to absorb minerals from the soil.
The emerging plant
Converts minerals into nourishment.
Stems and leaves stretch out to absorb the sun.
The result?
A flower.

Each human spirit
Is capable of producing
An extraordinary number
Of metaphorical flowers.

In a manner similar
To how a plant takes water, sun and minerals,
Each human spirit is nourished by their experience.
They learn.

Humanity's metaphorical blossoms?
Enlightened actions.
But an action,
Without the benefit of learning,
Absent the absorption of experience,
Is a weed.

Inertia

April 22, 2016

An object at rest
Is stuck.
Other energy
Must be introduced
To move it.

In life,
We are entangled
With many objects.
They push us up, down,
Left, right,
Backwards and forward.

When should one separate from one moment
In order to attach to another?
That is the dilemma!

This is how we define ourselves,
How we turn ourselves
Into something more
Than an object at rest.

Time Flies

May 21, 2016

Grains of sand
Slipped through my fingers.
My grandparents—gone.
My mother—gone.
My father—ill.
How long will he last?

My youthful generation—is now old.
Our babies—they have become adults.
And a new generation peeks out
From behind the bars of a crib.

Time passes.
But when we were young,
Time was as abundant
As grains of sand on the beach.

History is the story
Of sand that has passed
Between the fingers
Of people who are now almost forgotten.

Feel those grains pass
Between our fingers
It is time to realize
That we are next.

My Father's Passing
July 24, 2016

My dad lived to be ninety-four.
His life was rich.
He remained positive and alert
To the end.

But he is gone now.

What remains
Are my memories of him.
They span my life
And two-thirds of his.

My memories including stories of his childhood,
A Jewish boy growing up in Hitler's Germany.

The lessons he taught me
About courage, honesty and joy—
They also remain.

But my father is gone.

Spread Thin

August 25, 2016

The dissipation of my energy;
The absence of simplicity;
Competing moments where there is no competition;
No prioritization.

We like to think
We happen to life.
But that is a vain notion.
Life happens to us.

Sometimes,
We artfully
Carve with the grain.

But recently,
My efforts have been labored and
My vision of the world around me
Has lost it clarity.

Now is a time
In which I must find order.
I must pick up some pieces
And step forward.

Pride and Ignorance

October 3, 2016

I often ponder actions of my youth—
How I behaved.

Sometimes, I feel sheepish.
And other times, I feet shame—
Shame for the ignorance
And insensitivity
That obviously governed my behavior.

Now that I have aged,
I regard the pride I so often demonstrated,
With embarrassment,
With shame.

Each stage of life
Is really a cavalier foundation
For tomorrow's humility.

Oh—to replace pride with wisdom.

Our Essence

November 18, 2016

Each of us
Is involved in the process
Of making choices.

We establish patterns,
Repeat them,
And fine-tune them.

They are our sauce—
Our salvation—
Or our poison.

Sometimes, we improve our patterns,
Sometimes, we make them worse.
But we own them.
And they own us.

These patterns are the essence
Of who are,
Of what we are.

Winter Light

January 3, 2017

On a clear day,
The blue sky
Of winter
Does not make me warm.

It glares,
Making me uncomfortable
With its startling intensity.
But it doesn't make me warm.

I can look out the window
At the delicate crystal details
Of outdoor shapes and colors.

But in winter,
I take no solace
In the grandeur of the sun.
It just doesn't make me warm.

What is *It*?

February 12, 2017

Is *it* how happy you were,
How much fame you achieved,
Your wealth—your possessions,
Or how much pleasure
You enjoyed—or gave?

Is *it* what you created,
The peace you enjoyed,
Your laughter, knowledge,
Or the good and justice
You brought into the world?

Is *it* your nobility,
Your generosity, your fame, your piety,
Or how many you loved,
How many loved you,
Or the number of people
Who will mourn your passing?

What is the measure?
What gives life validity?
Is *it* written in stone?
Or is *it* just quietly reflected
In the gentle wind
That passes through the forest?

Meditation

February 21, 2017

Quiet.
Hear the silence.
The modern world is in abeyance.

I am doing nothing.
Not executing
The next empty task
Which would be aimed
At further constricting
Or restricting
Simplicity.

Completing that task
Would mean nothing.

But each of us always has a choice.
Do something without meaning
Or
Do nothing.

The empty cup awaits.

My Wife is Gone

March 20, 2017

My wife is gone.
Pancreatic cancer claimed her.
She fought it—
Brilliantly, bravely, with clear eyes.

But now, the one I love is gone.

The mother of my children,
The woman with whom I shared a bed,
My partner in every aspect of life.
A cook, a gardener, a painter—
A reader of books—
And a good person.
My best friend is gone.

I was a lucky man.
I am a lucky man.
I had forty-two years—
Of laughter, learning, adventure,
Exploring and sharing
This wondrous world.

My gentle and honest wife,
My best friend, my teacher,
And my pal
Is gone.

The Loss of a Best Friend

April 24, 2017

I was dutiful and true
And thought I was prepared.
I guess I was—
At least more than most.

One gets spoiled
By having someone there
Always.
Someone who listens
And understands
Or questions
Or laughs.

Now,
The silence
Is prominent.

A friend?
For what purpose?
Purpose was never a consideration.

It is a consideration now.
Discipline must replace that unknown purpose.

Disengaged—disconnected—ongoing.

Beginnings

May 22, 2017

Beginnings are a point,
Not a line.

The line only exists after
Other points have been added.

Seems simple.
But to become a point in a new line,
One must separate from the old line.

I am at a beginning.
One point
On an as yet undefined line.

There are so many possibilities.
It is actually breathtaking.
I inhale
The clean morning air.

I am refreshed.

Exploring One Moment

July 4, 2017

It is a truth that each of us will control and create
Our own unique moment
In time and space
In an infinite world.

As we explore that moment,
We are full of conjecture,
Ripe with interest—or maybe disinterest,
Brimming with beliefs—or not.

For what purpose?
I don't know.
But as I set out
To define my moment—
Who or what I am—
I am full of hope.

Capacity

July 25, 2017

Capacity is the room to expand—
To take on more.
It is the emptiness
That allows filling—completion—new functionality.

If a shelf is crowded,
There is little space
To add anything.
Something must be removed
To create capacity.

In life then,
You must be willing
To let go of the old
To have the capability
To add the new.

That is why we embrace emptiness.
It is the necessary prelude
To moving forward.

Change

August 12, 2017

One step forward.
Two steps back.
Perhaps.
But these are steps of change
And change is the essence of life.

Life is dynamic.
What applied today
May not apply tomorrow.
Seeking a plateau
In which there is no change
Is a fool's errand.
Because change happens—
It is life.
When we stop changing,
We die.

Embrace it.
Celebrate it.
Fear it, if you must.
But change is with us.

Sadness

September 5, 2017

My wife passed away
Six months ago.
I've dealt with it.
I've managed the bureaucracy,
Conducted the ceremonies
And changed many habits.

Now, I am moving into a different home.
I triaged our collection of things
Giving portions to the kids,
My sister, my brother, friends and charity.
I now pack the things that remain—
From our life, my life, into boxes.
I am dealing with it.

My home is for sale and
I purchased a condominium.

But as I try to figure out
Where I will place
My lovely little things
In my new home,
There is a sadness.

Challenging Realities

September 12, 2017

As a public sector CFO
During the final decade of my career,
I endured underfunded programs,
A collapsed economy, and
Poor communications
Between the executive and the council.
All the while,
I managed the bizarre political complexities
That go with controlling money.

But I had competent staff.
We operated with integrity,
Kept a positive focus
And held our heads high.

In the past three years,
I've lost my wife, my mother, my father,
My only aunt and my step-mother.
But the strength I developed as a financial executive
Served to prepare me
To deal with personal losses.

With the support of my family,
I've operated with integrity,
Kept a positive focus
And held my head high.

Getting Older

October 7, 2017

What part of getting older
Don't I get?
I am retired.
I take naps.
My energy is low.
And, since my wife died,
I live by myself
In a condominium.

And did I mention,
My body hurts?

I am sixty-eight years old
What part of getting older
Don't I get?

Quiet

January 21, 2017

Quiet is a form of art
That requires patience
And a lack of guile.

Modern times and quiet
Are contradictions.
Modern times are fol-de-rol—
To the nth degree.

Take a walk.
Breath through your nose.
Or simply sit
And gaze without intention.

This is a real foundation—
The only art form
That can
Save humanity.

Obituaries

February 10, 2017

I had never fully appreciated
The obituaries in the local paper.
I just didn't understand what they meant.

Then I learned
That when a life ended,
A life with countless details,
With family members grieving,
And memories imploding,
So many nuanced stories
Are replaced
By one column of newsprint
With a black and white photo
In an attempt
To somehow tie together
Decades of celebrations,
Feelings and accomplishments.

All of that love, joy and hope
Is morphed into a few paragraphs
Accompanied by sadness and pain.

Living Alone
January 10, 2018

For over forty years,
I shared a home with my wife.
She has passed now
And I am alone.

My life is good by most measures.
My home is comfortable.
I can afford food
And any other basics I need.

But now, living by myself,
I am without the company
Which was so easy
To take for granted.

When I get together
With friends or family
I speak more about myself
Than I had in the past.

A loneliness,
A new self-centeredness of sorts,
Has creeped into my personal equation.

Marsha

January 25, 2018

Marsha was an excellent painter.
I never could understand
Why she didn't pursue more recognition.
I guess she just didn't see herself as a painter.

She was a wonderful singer.
But she never wanted attention for that.
It wasn't that she didn't like to sing.
She just didn't consider herself a singer.

She could sew well,
Was a brilliant gardener and
A wonderful cook.
But she just didn't see herself
As a seamstress, a gardener, or a cook.

Marsha loved life,
Loved its beauty, its texture, and
Reveled in the opportunity
To explore its nuances.

For her,
It wasn't ever about her.
It was always about the beauty of life.

Putting things in Order

February 12, 2018

Human beings spend their lives,
Their resources, putting things in order.
There are many ways to organize,
So many approaches
For structuring our things and activities.
All of those approaches give a sense of certainty.

Order—however one defines it—
Gives a feeling of control,
Of balance, of harmony,
Of peace—
Even if it's an illusion.

Life is not chaos—
Or so we choose to believe.
Our proof?
Our collections are so nicely organized.

However,
When things do fall apart
In our day-to-day lives,
Our collections
Become disordered, threatening chaos.

(continued on next page)

(Putting Things in Order continued)

It is then that we transition towards new structures;
Arrange our things in new patterns
That will put an end to our emotional pandemonium.

Then,
After our little collections have been reordered,
Our assemblages put into neat rows,
We once again can sleep at night.

Criticism and Blame

April 12, 2018

The desire to criticize and blame,
To look at others' behavior and find fault,
Is an effort to escape ownership and accountability
By focusing negatively on others.
These actions
Lead away from resolution
Of anything.

They are destructive.

Understanding, analysis and compassion
Are ways to build bridges forward
Rather than tear them down.

Putting your arms around someone
Instead of hitting them
Makes this a better world.

Trying to understand a problem
By working with someone
Rather than criticizing them
Is a bridge to tomorrow.

Context

April 19, 2018

Ideas have meaning
Only within a context.
Solutions are found
After examining a context.
The beauty of an object exists
Primarily because of a context.

Those who study in isolation,
Who solve problems without understanding
The unique relationships and factors
That created the problem
Are merely playing a game.
Their conclusions are irrelevant.

Try to imagine the third note
Of Beethoven's fifth
Without envisioning the first two.

Try to be a friend to someone
Without understanding their fears or unique pain;
Without appreciating the history of their special joy.
That effort will amount to wind in the desert.

There is no insight without context.

Change is Constant

June 1, 2018

Tides go in.
Tides go out.
This appears to be
Simple repetition.

But as the water flows,
There is
Slow,
Steady,
Real
Change.

Sand moves.
Rocks are shaped.
Shorelines erode
And the change is constant.

Watch the water flow.
See the change.
Come to understand.

Learning #1

July 9, 2018

There is always new stuff to learn:
Life's evolutions,
Its permutations.
Its changes.

We must adapt.
There is no alternative.

Sometimes, we strive to learn.
Other times, it forces itself upon us.
We can learn by trial and error,
Analysis or
Shared insight from others.
There are many paths.

Many things,
Many ways and
Unlimited areas
In which to refine who we become,
How we live,
How we love and
What we experience.

Life is
Defined, refined and improved
By what we learn.

Navigation

August 11, 2018

Set a destination.
Motor out of the marina.
Raise the sails.
Choose a tack.
Then adjust for the current,
The tides and the wind.

Watch for debris.
Avoid shallow waters
And other boats.

Monitor your boat's equipment.
See the sites.
Watch the birds.
Look for dolphins
And maintain your course.

Sailing is a lot
Like everyday life.

Guilt

August 17, 2018

There is so much opulence in my home,
Such flexibility in how I live,
No hunger, no worry, no sleepless nights.
I feel guilty.

The history of the world
Is full of suffering,
Overflowing
With loneliness, famine and disease.

I am retired
And live in a safe, warm home,
Its walls covered with art.

After obtaining so much of what I wanted,
I wonder how and why
I escaped the pain.

It was all just too easy.

Technique

October 27, 2018

Technique is the learned *how*—
The magic
That ties intent and decision
Into quality of outcome.

Technique is the developed skill
To do a thing well—artfully if you will.
But,
If one chooses not to learn,
Technique is the short path to mediocrity.

I grind my coffee to a fine level,
Warm my press-pot with steaming hot water,
Waiting, then emptying it into the sink.
Then I transfer the ground coffee into the pot,
Fill it halfway with almost boiling water.
Wait once again—four minutes—
Before pressing down the plunger—
Oh, so slowly.

The coffee's flavor is rich,
Its scent aromatic.
My mug of coffee
Is a reward
For good technique.

Letting Go
November 18, 2018

Sand passed through my fingers.
I felt each grain
As it slid
Out of my grasp,
No longer a part of my life.

Emptiness
Is the beginning
Of all good things.

Letting go
Of parts of the past
Is not giving up.
It is opening the door
For change.

Things, people, habits and routines;
Change is a natural consequence of time of time.
But don't let go of everything.

Know what has meaning to you
And hold it close.

Layers of Lacquer

November 25, 2018

Carefully, patiently, cutting the wood.
Shaping its edges.
Each corner must be a tight fit.

Sanding,
And sanding,
And sanding.
From coarse to fine,
Seeking the flawless, smooth surface.

Applying the lacquer,
One thin coat at a time.
Letting it dry.
Carefully, gently, sanding once again.
And then,
One more thin coat of lacquer.

That was the past.
What has happened to craftsmanship?
Where has this execution of detail gone?

The satisfaction that came with skill and patience,
The joy of quality,
Of making things with one's own hands.

What has happened to us?

Misery

December 1, 2018

So much suffering.
So much poverty, hunger, sickness—
So many human beings living on the edge.

How distant that all is
From my warm comfortable home.
I live without hunger,
Without fear,
Without danger.

I am so insulated,
Enjoying life among the dilettantes
In a suffering world.

Forty million died from AIDS.
Billions live in squalid conditions—
They are hungry, cold and bereft.

And yet, many of us
Furiously peruse the web
Trying to identify
Some meaningless drivel
We might purchase
At a huge discount.

What emptiness and shame!

Oneness

December 24, 2018

Perform one task at a time—
Focus.
Do fewer things better—
Quality.
Select the right things—
Prioritize.
Think things through before acting—
Planning.
Learn from your mistakes—
Growing.
Find time to do nothing—
Meditate.
Have a value system and use it—
Foundation.
Understand your place in the world—
Humility.
Treat others with understanding—
Kindness.

Listen to the universe—
Tao.

Five years Passed

January 3, 2019

It's been almost five years
Since I retired.
How have I changed?
Or more truthfully,
How has life changed me?

A generation is gone.
My mother, my father, my step-mother and my aunt—
Gone.
My wife, passed on as well.
All of them—in the next world.

Me?
By myself, in this world.
Watching, listening, maybe learning
One day at a time.

The clock still chimes on the hour.
The sun still rises and sets.
But I am not the same.

I now sit alone.

Puzzles

January 21, 2019

Life is a series of puzzles.
Sometimes, one must assemble the pieces quickly.
Other times, speed is not helpful.

You can complete the puzzle rapidly
Or choose to be patient as you assemble the pieces,
Taking your time,
Trying to put it together perfectly
At the cost of time and missed opportunities.

When to go slowly?
Listen to your heart,
But learn from your mistakes.
Recognize when time has a price
And accept the consequences.

Take pride in the beauty
That you assemble.
Take solace from what you learn
When your puzzle isn't coming together.
Reflect on your vision.
Work with the pieces in front of you
Moving them around
In your mind's eye.

(continued on next page)

Poetry and Reflection

(Puzzles continued)

Recognize the limitations of your circumstances
But stretch yourself to also see the possibilities.
Make decisions.
Then put the pieces together
And appreciate your creation.

Letting Go

February 22, 2019

Letting go.
Memories, people, habits, things.

Doors will close behind you.
Always move forward while asking
What is next?
What will follow?

Things I've loved and
Things I've enjoyed
Are in the past.
As I move forward
Into the mist.

Life changes.
Embrace that fact.
Encourage opportunity
While retaining some caution.

But always remember,
You must be ready,
You have to be willing
To let go.

Chess

February 23, 2019

Life is a chessboard
Upon which we make decisive moves,
Using original strategies,
Creating personal outcomes.

The game of life is an opportunity
To accomplish much,
While wrestling with so many things
That are out of your control.
You must work intently
In spite of your previous careless moves.

Don't bring your queen out early.
Capture the center of the board,
And always look for an open file.
Those are rules to live by.

Always study the pieces on the board,
Think ahead
Anticipating your opponent's next move.
Then, when you are ready,
Move your piece.
Successful or not,
You own the outcome.
This is your life.
Be strategic.

Routines

May 23, 2019

Routines are
Repeating the same tasks
Performed in the same way
On a regular basis.

Routines can simplify
Those parts of our lives
That are most tedious.

They can be wonderful.
Enabling us to focus upon
Those things which are most important.

(Or, they can cause us to ignore opportunities
For knowledge, experience and growth).

Know your routines.
Know what they do for you
(And what they do to you).

A Kaleidoscope

June 7, 2019

Life is a constantly changing kaleidoscope
Offering uninterrupted apparitions
Of smell, taste, sound, touch and sight.

There are so many diverse tantalizing moments—
The scent of roast beef or pumpkin pie
Emanating from an oven;
A mountain peeking through clouds
Early on a cool morning;
The mournful cry of a dove;
A ferry horn blasting through the fog;
Another person's touch; or
The delicate taste of freshly baked blackberry pie.

Sensory events are all around us.
We pay attention to some of them
And remember a few.

But so many special sensual opportunities
Just pass us by
Without our notice.

Quel dommage!

Like an Onion

August 22, 2019

Something learned, something experienced;
Sometimes by choice, other-times by fate or fortune;
Joy, humility, love and loss—
They all becomes layers of who we are.

Yes,
We are like an onion,
A composite of many layers.

Each of us develops over time
Into a unique, personal multi-faceted mélange
Of habits, memories, biases and personal wisdom.

Understanding

September 18, 2019

Watch, listen, absorb.
Then, consider, digest and formulate
How you will move forward.

Listen to your heart.
Remember your experiences—
Both the things that worked
And the things that didn't.

Review what you were told
By the people whom you respect.
Remember the errors you made,
And the lessons you learned from them.
Recall—the what, how and why of your successes.

Understanding is like sunlight
Coming through the clouds.
Some days it arrives quickly.
Other days it does not appear.

Be patient when you need to be
And always listen to your heart.

Possibilities

September 25, 2019

Life should be a search for possibilities.
What might happen?
What door could have been hidden—
Left unopened in the fog of being?

Definition should not be just an outline
Of normal patterns.
Definition should allow the exploration
Of space and opportunities
That are not yet readily apparent.

Look out into the fog!
See the vague shape that was almost hidden.
Try to explore what is undiscovered
Without desecrating the past.

Adventure can be subtle.
Move forward
Into the unknown.

Yom Kippur 2019

October 9, 2019

The Day of Atonement
Always brings the questions:
What to atone for?
Where to grow?

Is the ritual meaningful?
Should I eat?
Shall I pray?
Do I beg forgiveness—
From God?
From others?

I have been given so much.
Have I been appreciative?
Have I given back—sufficiently?

Where do I go from here?
Left foot, right foot;
Left foot, right foot;
Always that pattern.
Where does it lead?
For what purpose?

(continued on next page)

Poetry and Reflection

(Yom Kippur 2019 continued)

The perennial *why*
Is the shadow that overwhelms everything.
It always has.

But today, one must confront that *why*
Knowing that without an inner search
One ends up living in a wasteland.

Patterns

November 10, 2019

I depend upon patterns.
They help me navigate time.
Building, using, enjoying and resting—
All done within comfortable patterns.

I am married to a person who doesn't live by patterns.
She is a woman driven by objectives.
But both of our methods of life
Are driven by values.

Galina lives in what seems to be a random fashion,
Waking each day,
Doing what needs to be done,
And working to achieve
What is in her heart.
But there is a consistency—
A lyrical string that ties the beads of her efforts
Into a magic necklace of purpose.

This is a different and refreshing break
From what I've known.

What Would Have Happened If

December 1, 2019

What would have happened
If I had only prepared
Or had not prepared;
If I had left early
Or had not left later.
Life is full of dynamic consequences
Of lightly considered actions.

Sometimes we feel,
After proper consideration,
That we can anticipate the future—
Sometimes we feel like we can.

We act based upon assumed probabilities.
But life is not a simple mathematical equation.
Its variables extend beyond our imagination.

We are left depending upon fortune, luck or God.
Call it what you will.
You just don't know
What will happen—
What could have happened.

The Pieces

December 25, 2019

All chess games begin with thirty-two pieces.
But as a game proceeds,
The arrangement of pieces on the chessboard
Becomes so complex
That a solution seems unfathomable.

But look at the board a little longer.
A pattern will emerge.

Think ahead.
What are your options?
Anticipate possible responses and outcomes.
Then,
Make one move at a time.

Slower

January 20, 2020

When I was young,
I made decisions quickly.
Turning on a dime,
I often was right!

As I have aged,
I've learned to take my time,
To understand what I am dealing with
And to examine its context.

I now try to find out
Who's affected,
What are the options
And consider the pros and cons
Of each strategy—
Before I act.

As a result,
I spend less time
Looking back at my actions
Saying *shit*.

(continued on next page)

Poetry and Reflection

(Slower continued)

Time is a valuable commodity
Which you should never be afraid to use.
And while you must never be afraid to act,
You should try to understand
What you are doing,
Why you are doing it and
What the impacts might be
Before you act.

The Art of How

March 30, 2020

We generally focus on *what*.
Wisdom is often perceived
As the art of selecting
The best *what*.

But quality does not come from *what*.
Quality comes from *how*.

What leads to quality?

Learning the fundamental skills,
Practicing and refining the appropriate nuances,
Seeing, listening and responding
With the purpose of creating excellence.

Patience, diligence, and thoroughness
Employed while responding to the nature
of the medium in which you work:
That is the art of *how*.

Craftsmanship, technique and quality—
These are different faces of the same promise.

Chaos of Sadness and Light

March 10, 2020

Things are happening
Always—
All around—
A chaos of sadness and light.

We are part
Of the systems of nature
As well as the systems of humanity.
Each individual system creates richness—
Sometimes.
And other times, it spawns
Sadness, despair or emptiness.

We are aware of
A multitude of systems.
Some, we admire.
Others, we dislike or fear.
And there are many we choose to ignore.

But we will always struggle to comprehend
How all of these moving parts can fit together—
And why?

Our universe is a symphony
Of harmonic dissonance,
A chaos of sadness and light.

Validation

April 8, 2020

Some people want adventure.
Others pursue pleasure.
Many work to bathe in luxury.
The pure aspire to high moral ground
While hedonists seek out sensual delight
And those who are confused just chase an identity.

There are so many quests.
But at the end of the day,
All of us are after validation.
We want acknowledgement
Of attaining
What it is, what it was—
That we seek, that we sought.

During our lives, we pursue different things
In different ways.
But each of us wishes for completion
In the form of some sort of affirmation,
An acknowledgment from those we respect.

We want validation.

Appreciation

May 25, 2020

There is a lot of pain in this world.
People are hungry, cold and alone.
Billions live under difficult conditions
In fear of threats I have never faced.

I don't know hunger.
I haven't seen danger.
My world is safe
And my needs are met.

Why?
What did I do to stave off all of that pain?
How is it that I am not hungry, cold or afraid?
Why do I live in comfort and security?

I don't know.
But, at a minimum,
I need to be aware of,
And have compassion for,
The other 98% of humanity.

Randomness

June 7, 2020

Embrace the randomness of life.
Doors come along
When you least expect them.
Walk through them.

Other doors will close before you can enter.
Their locks engaging.
Move on.

Life is transitory.
There is no map.
We don't know what's next.
But it awaits us.

Keep moving.
Recognize what is special.
Laugh, cry, learn, and enjoy.

What is Wisdom?

June 17, 2020

What is wisdom?
I am certain it's not just about thinning grey hair—
Or walking around expressing ponderous thoughts.

Prerequisites for wisdom
Are peacefulness and kindness;
Honesty, faithfulness and caring.
And yes, knowing when to act.
And of course, the ability to make decisions—
Decisions that are not based on personal benefit.

Wisdom includes the ability to see into the future—
And understand the ramifications of today's actions
Upon tomorrow.

In its infancy, wisdom is the willingness to learn
While acting with compassion and humility
And being willing to admit an error.

Achieving wisdom may be difficult,
But this quality is the essence
Of what humanity needs.

What is Selfishness?

June 17, 2020

Selfishness has many flavors—
So many ways in which a person can think of himself
or herself first.

Selfish people are arrogant and self-righteous.
Their behavior is not driven by understanding
But by greed.
Their actions are focused on the short-term
And their behavior is often mean or cruel.

Selfish people are not happy.
They feel that life has left them short-changed.
So, they grab for themselves first.

Yes, selfishness is the lack wisdom.

Learning #2

August 20, 2020

Every time I think things have settled down
And have begun to feel comfortable,
I discover
Something I need to learn.

This occurs
After I trip and fall—
Sometimes more than once.
What was that, I say to myself.
Oh yes, an opportunity to learn.

I could call these instances
Discovering a blind spot
Or understanding my own stupidity.
But whatever name I give this phenomenon,
The need for understanding is clear.
And once I understand what has happened,
I can change how I operate
In my journey through life.

The magic of a good life—
Is stopping in one's tracks
(Usually because of an error)
And adjusting course.

(continued on next page)

(Learning #2 continued)

Keep in mind,
That when you stop learning,
You haven't stopped making errors,
You've just stopped benefitting from them.

Or perhaps, you are dead.

Discovery

August 28, 2020

Life is a process of discovery.
We make mistakes—
And we learn!
We research—
And we learn!
Someone tells us something new—
And we learn!
Discoveries all!

Those discoveries can come from good things,
Bad things,
Or things that everyone else knows.
The source makes little difference—
As long as we are enriched.

Things we should have known,
Things we forgot and
Things we didn't want to learn—
All discoveries.

This continues
Until that day
We slip away—
Perhaps to make
Our biggest discovery.

New Things

September 15, 2020

The smell, texture and shine;
The novelty, functionality and design;
The sensations these all represent—
While unwrapping something new.

It makes us feel so good.
How did we get along without it?
Why didn't we buy it sooner?
We are so contented.

And the cost was reasonable—
We could afford it, I guess.
We needed it—I think.
We certainly wanted it.

The pleasure of a new thing envelops us.
Until
One day,
It becomes old.

La Shanah Tovah

September 29, 2020

It has always seemed appropriate
That the conclusion of the Jewish new year,
Yom Kippur,
Occurs near my birthday.

Each year on Yom Kippur,
I look back
Trying to recognize
And focus upon
My errors and faults.
How do I need to grow?
How have I fallen short of what I should be?
Then, shortly after that,
I celebrate the anniversary of my birth.

Now, approaching completion
Of my seventy-first year of life,
Facing my seventy-second year,
I again visualize the growth
That I must embrace.
Don't be so reactive.
Listen first.
Take care of my health.
And think more about others.

Why do these goals seem so familiar?

Understanding and Actions

October 9, 2020

It cuts through confusion
Like a knife slices through butter.
It transverses anger
Like fish swims through water.
It brightens dark feelings
Like the sun lights up the day.

Take your time.
Consider the person,
Their experiences,
And their tendencies.
Examine the context.
See the issue clearly.

Then pause
And come to an understanding.

Only after this should you act.

The Juxtaposition of Courage and Wisdom

October 15, 2020

I was born brave,
Full of valor,
Always listening to my heart
And acting on its intentions—
Undaunted.

The bravery and foolhardy actions I demonstrated
Belong to the young.
As I grew older, I gained perspective
On how naive and foolhardy I was;
How shallow;
How unaware.

Getting older may be leading to wisdom,
But it has also forced me to try to comprehend
What I have been given
And to consider the important questions:
Why has life been so easy?
What did I do to deserve this?
What must I do to justify it?

Rather than being a moment of victory,
Wisdom offers a lesson in humility.

Different Formulas

November 20, 2020

I. Scientists reach different conclusions.
    a. Alternate formulas
    b. In which different assumptions are applied,
    c. While different data sources are utilized,
    d. And variables are weighed differently,
    e. Will produce divergent conclusions, and
    f. Result in accusations of incompetence.

II. And people see things differently as well.
    a. Men and women with varying levels of
        intelligence and education,
    b. Who have different belief systems,
    c. And base judgement on different experiences,
    d. Will analyze what they see differently,
    e. Reach different conclusions, and
    f. Accuse one another of ignorance

Simple Moral:
Try to understand the other person's belief systems.
Appreciate their different life experience.
Who knows?
You might be able to understand that person.

Wisdom

December 6, 2020

As a young man,
I hoped that when I aged,
I would become wise.

But I wasn't sure what wisdom was.
I knew that Solomon was wise
When he suggested cutting the baby into two.
And I knew that the great mystics were wise
When they shared insights
That were difficult to understand.

But now,
As an older person,
I think I might be beginning to understand
What wisdom is.

Wisdom is the humility to question your role;
The recognition of when action is required;
The judgement to recognize what needs to be done;
The understanding of
How your actions will affect others;
And the courage to act, or not,
Depending upon the circumstances.

Now that I believe I know what wisdom is,
My challenge is to act wisely.

Do Who We Are

February 21, 2021

There are the things I want to do;
The things I have to do;
The things I'm forced to do;
And those that I like to do.

And then,
Of course,
There is what I will do.

That last item describes who I am.
It represents how my reality has been shaped
In the face of contexts and opportunities.

Change

February 24, 2021

Change is a machine
That chews up your past,
Then spits out the future.

The past and the future
Only come together
At moments
That quickly disappear
Into clouds of dust.

Sometimes, we call those moments *the present*.
Other times, we call them *dreams*.

The End of the Beginning of the End

March 14, 2021

This journal
Began more than seven years ago.
Poetry and Reflection speaks to changes
As they occurred
To a man
Who was thrilled
To be finished with his career.

The journal is full now
With once-a-month admissions
And the perceptions of a slowly aging soul.

The ride was certainly not
What I had anticipated.
It was bumpier than I had hoped.
But it has been rich.
And for that,
I can only be grateful.

www.ingramcontent.com/pod-product-compliance
Lightning Source LLC
Chambersburg PA
CBHW071200120626
46546CB00006B/2352